Developing and Evaluating Multi-Agency Partnerships

D0274127

In recent years government initiatives such as Sure Start, Extended Schools and Every Child Matters have been significant in the promotion of an agenda to create collaborative working environments and introduce multi-agency practice into a range of child-centred settings. *Developing and Evaluating Multi-Agency Partnerships* provides advice and guidance for managers and leaders responsible for overseeing multi-agency workings in these settings, providing a self-evaluation framework to help improve the quality and effectiveness of multi-agency relationships.

The valuable tools and templates within this book will:

- explain the importance of self-evaluation;
- provide a framework for self-evaluation via a step-by-step guide;
- link multi-agency practice with improving the Every Child Matters outcomes;
- suggest best practice for gathering multi-agency evidence;
- give guidance on building a portfolio of evidence and achieving external recognition.

The self-evaluation framework provided in this book meets the requirements of the Children's Workforce standards and Ofsted requirements for effective partnerships. A highly practical handbook, this is essential reading for all those who are implementing or improving a multi-agency partnership in their setting. To improve the effectiveness of this resource, additional resources are downloadable in customisable form from www. routledgeteachers.com/resources/fulton.

Rita Cheminais is an author, keynote speaker and trainer on ECM, a School Improvement Partner and a freelance education consultant with Every Child Matters (ECM) Solutions. She can be contacted at: admin@ ecm-solutions.org.uk and www.ecm-solutions.org.uk.

Developing and Evaluating Multi-Agency Partnerships

A practical toolkit for schools and children's centre managers

RITA CHEMINAIS

Routledge
Taylor & Francis Group

LONDON AND NEW YORK

First published 2010
by Routledge
2 Park Square, Milton Park, Abingdon, Oxon OX14 4RN

Simultaneously published in the USA and Canada
by Routledge
270 Madison Ave, New York, NY 10016

Routledge is an imprint of the Taylor & Francis Group, an informa business

© 2010 Rita Cheminais

Typeset in Sabon by Wearset Ltd, Boldon, Tyne and Wear
Printed and bound in Great Britain by CPI Antony Rowe, Chippenham,
Wiltshire

British Library Cataloguing in Publication Data
A catalogue record for this book is available from the British Library

Library of Congress Cataloging-in-Publication Data
Cheminais, Rita
Developing and evaluating multi-agency partnerships: a practical toolkit for schools and children's centre managers/Rita Cheminais
p. cm.
Includes bibliographical references and index.
1. Educational evaluation–Great Britain–Handbooks, manuals, etc. 2. Education–Standards–Great Britain–Handbooks, manuals, etc. 3. School management and organization–Great Britain–Handbooks, manuals, etc. 4. Interagency coordination–Great Britain–Handbooks, manuals, etc. I. Title.
LB2822.75.C466 2010
379.1'580941–dc22   2009014396

ISBN10: 0-415-55657-0 (hbk)
ISBN10: 0-415-55658-9 (pbk)
ISBN10: 0-203-86912-5 (ebk)

ISBN13: 978-0-415-55657-6 (hbk)
ISBN13: 978-0-415-55658-3 (pbk)
ISBN13: 978-0-203-86912-3 (ebk)

Contents

Illustrations

Figures

Tables

Boxes

Multi-agency self-evaluation grids

Portfolio checklists

Portfolio evidence sheets

Acknowledgements

This book would not have become a reality without the support of my commissioning editor, Annamarie Kino, and Sophie Thomson, editorial assistant at Routledge Education.

I have to thank all those wonderful children's workforce practitioners, leaders and managers of early-years settings, children's centres and schools that I have been privileged to meet on my travels throughout the country, who have inspired and encouraged me to produce this essential, much-needed resource.

I trust that all those who use this book will find it an invaluable resource, and enjoy working their way through the nine aspects of multi-agency working.

Abbreviations

CAF	common assessment framework
CPD	continuing professional development
CRB	Criminal Records Bureau
DCSF	Department for Children, Schools and Families
ECM	Every Child Matters
EYFS	Early Years Foundation Stage
INSET	in-service education and training
LA	local authority
NCSCL	National College for School and Children's Leadership
NPQH	National Professional Qualification for Headteachers
NPQICL	National Professional Qualification in Integrated Centre Leadership
NSF	National Service Framework
Ofsted	Office for Standards in Education, Children's Services and Skills
PRU	pupil referral unit
QISP	Quality Improvement Support Programme
SEF	self-evaluation form
SIP	School Improvement Partner
TAC	Team Around the Child
TDA	Training and Development Agency for Schools

How to use this resource

This book is designed to support all those involved in leading, managing and evaluating multi-agency working in a range of education settings and children's services. In addition, the resource enables leaders and managers in early-years settings, children's centres, schools, academies and pupil referral units (PRUs) to gather evidence that will contribute to meeting the ten elements of each of the nine aspects relating to multi-agency working.

Each chapter in this book focuses on a stage in the multi-agency self-evaluation process: auditing current practice; action planning; and building a portfolio of evidence. Education settings and services can use the evidence gathered to contribute to the Ofsted (Office for Standards in Education, Children's Services and Skills) self-evaluation form (SEF), as well as gaining external recognition beyond the inspection process, through the achievement of an award for good and outstanding practice in multi-agency working.

The timescale for an education setting or service to work towards meeting all of the nine aspects of multi-agency working will vary according to their context and capacity to improve. The majority of education settings and services find one year to be an appropriate length of time for gathering all the necessary evidence. A setting or service may choose to focus on all nine aspects at once, or on three aspects of multi-agency working per term.

This book provides a step-by-step guide for all those wishing to take the journey towards developing and improving the quality and effectiveness of the multi-agency working taking place within their setting or service. It contains all the necessary tools required to engage in the multi-agency self-evaluation process.

The self-evaluation grids, action plan, portfolio of evidence checklists, and resources in the Appendix are available to download from the Routledge Education website.

Irrespective of whether an education setting or service decides to register for the multi-agency award, the collaborative process of self-evaluation contributes immensely to strengthening teamwork, and to achieving better outcomes for children and young people. It is a cost-effective resource to use as it creates little, if any, extra work in the evidence-gathering process, because it is part of every day multi-agency practice. It makes the self-evaluation process for multi-agency working manageable, rewarding and worthwhile.

Overall, this excellent value resource provides leaders and managers responsible for multi-agency working in education settings and children's services with a robust tool for benchmarking their integrated multi-agency practice. It also offers a rigorous and consistent approach to judging the effectiveness and impact of collaborative partnership working on improving outcomes for children and young people.

Introduction

According to the government, multi-agency partnership working is about different services, agencies and teams of professionals and other staff working together to provide the services that fully meet the needs of children, young people and their parents or carers.

The government's initiatives, such as Sure Start, Extended Schools and Every Child Matters (ECM) have been significant key drivers in promoting collaborative, joined-up multi-agency working to support a range of education settings in improving children and young people's well-being and life chances. The Children Act 2004 further strengthened the requirement for agencies and services to work together more closely in multi-disciplinary teams in order to safeguard and improve the ECM outcomes.

Schools and other education settings cannot be expected to meet all the requirements of the ECM agenda alone. Leaders and managers in education settings appreciate the added-value contributions that multi-agency practitioners make to their ongoing work in promoting pupil well-being.

The government has been keen to promote integrated multi-agency working, because it enables:

- the five ECM well-being outcomes to be enhanced and improved;
- the pooling of multi-agency practitioners' expertise, knowledge, skills and resources to occur, which leads to more efficient and effective working;
- children and young people to reach their optimum potential through the removal of barriers to learning and participation;
- early intervention and preventative work to take place in order to address any problems immediately;

- services to be tailored and personalised according to the aspirations and needs of the child or young person;
- a holistic approach to be adopted in meeting all the needs of the child or young person;
- teachers to focus on their core role of teaching in order to facilitate children's and young people's learning.

Having a team of multi-agency practitioners working directly with children and young people – for example, within a school or children's centre – brings extra responsibility and accountability for leaders and managers, such as:

- managing a larger children's workforce team;
- endeavouring to keep track of all the different multi-agency practitioners and professionals working with children, young people and their parents or carers;
- overseeing service level agreements, policy and procedures for partnership working;
- getting to grips with the complexities of children's trusts, brokering and commissioning services;
- monitoring, evaluating and assuring the quality in terms of the effectiveness and impact of multi-agency partnership working/ Team around the Child (TAC) within an education setting.

This resource, *Developing and Evaluating Multi-Agency Partnerships: A Practical Toolkit for Schools and Children's Centre Managers*, offers the ideal tool for evaluating the key aspects of multi-agency working. It offers leaders and managers of education settings, children's centres and children's services a resource that meets the requirements of the National Service Framework (NSF) quality standards, in addition to the core standards for multi-agency working. It also complements the Early Years Quality Improvement Support Programme (QISP) aspects of helping to develop practitioner learning and facilitating partnerships for learning and development.

The self-evaluation framework within the book enables robust evidence to be gathered that demonstrates good practice in the nine aspects of multi-agency working, which covers:

1. policy, procedures and legal responsibilities;
2. the working environment;
3. leadership and management;
4. communication and information sharing;
5. inter-professional relationships and roles;
6. team working;
7. resources;
8. working with service users/clients;
9. professional learning.

The nine aspects of the multi-agency self-evaluation framework complement and align with the Ofsted inspection requirements for early-years settings, schools, children's centres and local authority (LA) children's services. The self-evaluation process will also enable leaders and managers to gather evidence that responds to the following questions:

- To what extent are the multi-agency services making a difference?
- Why have the particular multi-agency services been established?
- How well are the multi-agency services being used?
- Who are the key multi-agency partners and how effective are relationships between them?
- Who is accountable for the multi-agency services being delivered?
- How is the work of multi-agency practitioners being monitored and evaluated?
- How accessible are the multi-agency services for service users/clients?

This book acts as the essential handbook to guide education settings and services throughout the entire multi-agency self-evaluation process, irrespective of whether they wish to proceed towards achieving a national award.

This resource is unique and groundbreaking because it is the first one of its kind specifically focused on evaluating multi-agency partnerships, and has the potential to offer an award, in recognition of good practice in multi-agency working. You can download all the necessary resources from the following website: www.routledge. com/education.

Further information about registering for the award process, purchasing support, consultancy and external assessment is available by emailing admin@ecm-solutions.org.uk or visiting the website: www.ecm-solutions.org.uk.

1

The origin and benefits of the multi-agency self-evaluation process

The origin of the multi-agency self-evaluation framework and process

The multi-agency self-evaluation framework and process arose in response to a number of head teachers' requests for a robust evidence-gathering tool that would enable them to demonstrate and gain external recognition, beyond Ofsted, specifically for their good practice in multi-agency working.

A journal article that I had published in January 2009, entitled 'Getting together', became the trigger that eventually prompted the development and launch of the multi-agency self-evaluation framework and process nationally.

The purpose of the multi-agency self-evaluation framework and process

The self-evaluation framework for multi-agency working is designed to enable leaders and managers in a range of education settings and LA children's services to meet the government's requirements in relation to having highly skilled and knowledgeable children's workforce practitioners working directly with children and young people.

The multi-agency self-evaluation framework that supports the evidence-gathering process is aligned with the children's workforce core standards, particularly the one related to multi-agency working. It complements the Early Years QISP and the quality standards in the NSF. It also contributes valuable evidence for the Ofsted SEF. This ensures that it meets all the necessary accountability requirements placed on education settings, which includes children's centres and children's services.

Where and when the multi-agency self-evaluation framework can be used

The multi-agency self-evaluation framework and process can be utilised in early-years settings, children's centres, mainstream primary and secondary schools, special schools, academies and PRUs. It also has the potential to be used in LA children's services.

When to use the multi-agency self-evaluation framework and process is very much dependent on a setting's or service's current context and the starting point from which they are approaching multi-agency working. An education setting or children's service is in a stronger position to engage with the multi-agency self-evaluation process when:

- an Ofsted inspection has identified multi-agency/partnership working as being a good or outstanding feature;
- the setting or service is already delivering successful and effective extended services as part of the core offer;
- the capacity exists among practitioners in the setting or service to meet all the elements of the nine aspects of multi-agency working at the embedded level on the self-evaluation framework;
- there is a genuine, agreed willingness and commitment among key stakeholders within the setting or service to fully engage with the multi-agency self-evaluation process.

The pre-requisites for engaging with the multi-agency self-evaluation process

The following pre-requisites act as the necessary guiding principles for positive engagement with the multi-agency self-evaluation process:

- the leader or manager of the education setting or service has shared their vision for productive multi-agency working with stakeholders;

- a presentation has been delivered within the education setting or service, which raises staff and governors' awareness about the benefits and purpose of engaging in the multi-agency self-evaluation process;
- there is a high level of trust and mutual respect among multi-agency practitioners and staff within the service/education setting;
- the contributions that multi-agency practitioners make to improving children's and young people's well-being is acknowledged and valued by the education setting/service;
- team work and collaborative practice are a strength of the education setting or service;
- there is a strong focus on continual improvement in the aspect of multi-agency working within the education setting/service;
- there is a designated senior member of staff – who has sufficient quality time to perform the role – that is responsible for overseeing the entire multi-agency self-evaluation process within the education setting or service;
- a working party or task group is established to assist with the evidence-gathering process towards meeting all nine aspects of multi-agency working;
- time is made available for the working party/task group to meet at least once every half term with the designated senior member of staff, in order to review progress towards meeting the nine aspects of multi-agency working;
- those education settings or services that wish to gain an award for their good practice in multi-agency working sign a contract of agreement to commission consultancy and external assessment from Every Child Matters (ECM) Solutions.

The benefits of engaging with the multi-agency self-evaluation process

The main benefits of participating in the multi-agency self-evaluation process are noted below.

- The education setting or service will have a rich source of evidence which demonstrates how they are meeting all the necessary core and quality standards relating to multi-agency working and effective service delivery.

- The education setting or service will be well placed for meeting any local authority or Ofsted inspection accountability requirements.
- It engages a diverse range of stakeholders in the process, which strengthens the commitment to integrated, collaborative multi-agency working.
- It is an invaluable tool for building the capacity among multi-agency practitioners in order to further develop integrated partnership working.
- It offers the potential to achieve an award in recognition of good practice in multi-agency working.
- It helps to identify and disseminate best-practice in multi-agency working locally and nationally.
- It complements the Training and Development Agency for Schools (TDA) *School Improvement Planning Framework* module, *Beyond the Classroom*, as well as their *Extended School Toolkit for Governors*, and the Department for Children, Schools and Families (DCSF)/National Strategies Early Years QISP.
- It can be used in conjunction with the National College for School and Children's Leadership (NCSCL) online ECM Leadership Direct's resource section on multi-agency partnership working.
- It supports the aspects of multi-agency partnership working that feature in the National Professional Qualification in Integrated Centre Leadership (NPQICL) and in the National Professional Qualification for Headteachers (NPQH).
- It supports the Ofsted SEF in relation to the contribution of services and the impact they have on improving children's and young people's ECM well-being outcomes.
- It complements the Children's Workforce Development Councils (CWDC) One Children's Workforce Framework for Children's Trusts.

If, after reading this first chapter, you consider that you meet the majority of the pre-requisites for commencing the multi-agency self-evaluation process, then move on to the next chapter, which will describe how to use the framework.

2

Overview of the multi-agency self-evaluation process, auditing and action planning

There are four key stages in the multi-agency self-evaluation process.

Stage 1: auditing current multi-agency practice. This stage entails an audit of multi-agency policy and practice being undertaken by the designated senior member of staff, in partnership with those who are on the working party or task group, using the multi-agency self-evaluation framework. This will enable a view to be formed as to whether current policy and practice is *emergent* (in the early stages), *developing* (work is in progress) or *embedded* (fully in place), in relation to all the elements for each of the nine aspects of multi-agency working.

Stage 2: action planning. This stage entails producing an action plan, which identifies the aspects and elements of multi-agency working that require further action in order to move them from *emergent* and *developing* to become *embedded*.

Stage 3: collecting evidence and monitoring progress. This stage entails carrying out the necessary actions and activities in order to improve – and meet all the elements of – the nine aspects of multi-agency working. A portfolio is compiled which brings together all the evidence required to meet the nine aspects of multi-agency working. Regular and ongoing monitoring of progress provides the necessary checks and balances in the multi-agency self-evaluation process.

Stage 4: evaluation and assessment. This is the final stage in reviewing and reflecting on the overall multi-agency self-evaluation process. For those education settings or services who wish to achieve an award in recognition of their good practice in multi-agency working, it also entails undergoing an external assessment on-site for half a day, and an off-site assessment of the multi-agency portfolio of evidence. Figure 2.1 illustrates the stages of the multi-agency self-evaluation process.

The multi-agency self-evaluation framework

The self-evaluation framework focuses on nine aspects of multi-agency working. These are:

1. policy, procedures and legal responsibilities;
2. the working environment;
3. leadership and management;
4. communication and information sharing;
5. inter-professional relationships and roles;
6. team working;
7. resources;
8. working with service users/clients;
9. professional learning.

Each aspect of multi-agency working has ten elements or evidence descriptors. These form the framework for the entire multi-agency evidence-gathering process. The self-evaluation grids are included in this book, and they can be downloaded at: www.routledge.com/education.

The multi-agency self-evaluation grids support the audit and evidence-gathering stages. Each of the nine aspects of multi-agency working and their ten evidence descriptors, enable an education setting or service to make valid and consistent judgements about their multi-agency working policy and practice.

The evidence descriptors for each of the nine multi-agency working aspects take into account the government's expectations for developing an effective, highly skilled and knowledgeable children's workforce, equipped to meet the needs of children and young people in the twenty-first century.

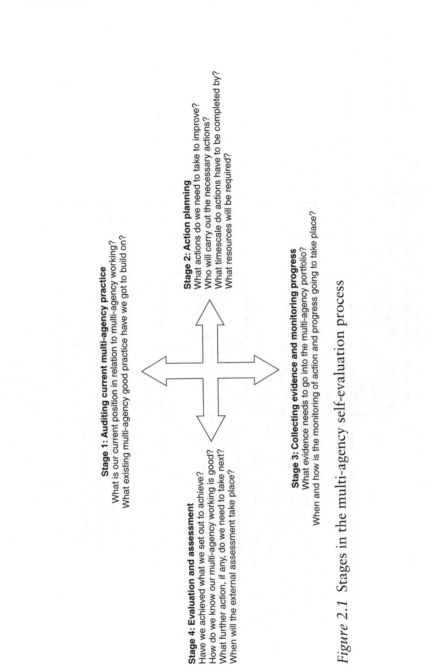

Stage 1: Auditing current multi-agency practice
What is our current position in relation to multi-agency working?
What existing multi-agency good practice have we got to build on?

Stage 2: Action planning
What actions do we need to take to improve?
Who will carry out the necessary actions?
What timescale do actions have to be completed by?
What resources will be required?

Stage 4: Evaluation and assessment
Have we achieved what we set out to achieve?
How do we know our multi-agency working is good?
What further action, if any, do we need to take next?
When will the external assessment take place?

Stage 3: Collecting evidence and monitoring progress
What evidence needs to go into the multi-agency portfolio?
When and how is the monitoring of action and progress going to take place?

Figure 2.1 Stages in the multi-agency self-evaluation process

1a Policy, procedures and legal requirements

Evidence descriptor	Emergent (early stages) – ✓ or ✗	Developing (in progress) – ✓ or ✗	Embedded (fully in place) – ✓ or ✗	Evaluative evidence/impact on pupils' ECM well-being outcomes
There is a policy for partnership working in place, which reflects the NSF.				
Multi-agency practitioners follow the correct safeguarding policy and child protection procedures.				
Multi-agency practitioners have regard to the setting's equalities and diversity/equal opportunities policy				
Multi-agency practitioners follow the setting's health and safety policy and procedures.				
There is an inter-professional partnership working agreement in place, which all multi-agency practitioners follow.				
Service level agreements are in place for all the services/agencies, organisations working with the setting.				
Procedures for raising concerns, referral, assessment, commissioning and terminating services/provision are clear and understood.				

The procedures for initiating and engaging with the CAF process are clear and utilised effectively by all the relevant staff and multi-agency practitioners/ professionals.		
All multi-agency practitioners understand and follow the agreed procedures for recording, reporting, monitoring and evaluating the impact and outcomes of their interventions and provision.		
All practitioners who are working directly with children and young people have enhanced CRB.		

2a The working environment

Evidence descriptor	Emergent (early stages) – ✔ or ✗	Developing (in progress) – ✔ or ✗	Embedded (fully in place) – ✔ or ✗	Evaluative evidence/impact on pupils' ECM well-being outcomes
There is an inclusive culture and ethos existing in the setting which welcomes all multi-agency practitioners.				
A pleasant, safe, sound-proofed, clean and well maintained working environment is provided for multi-agency practitioners within the setting.				
Appropriate facilities, access to administrative support, internet/computer access, a telephone and secure filing cabinets are available to multi-agency practitioners in their work area within the setting.				
There is a dedicated base for multi-agency practitioners to use within the setting, which is accessible and welcoming to service users and staff within the setting.				
Multi-agency practitioners are welcome in the setting's staff room and are included in any social events.				
There is discreet access to the multi-agency base within the setting for parents/carers and members of the community.				

Developing and Evaluating Multi-Agency Partnerships. A Practical Toolkit for Schools and Children's Centre Managers, Routledge Education © Rita Cheminais 2010.

Multi-agency practitioners take responsibility for any specialist equipment and the facilities used within their working area in the setting.			
The multi-agency base in the setting has secure storage facilities for any specialist equipment and computer hardware.			
Multi-agency practitioners know who to report any repairs or room maintenance issues to within the setting.			
Multi-agency practitioners understand and apply safe working practices within the setting.			

3a Leadership and management

Evidence descriptor	Emergent (early stages) – ✓ or ✗	Developing (in progress) – ✓ or ✗	Embedded (fully in place) – ✓ or ✗	Evaluative evidence/impact on pupils' ECM well-being outcomes
There is a designated senior member of staff in the setting who oversees multi-agency partnerships and acts as a point of contact for these external practitioners.				
Multi-agency practitioners have been involved in the setting's improvement planning process.				
Multi-agency practitioners know and are clear about the setting's improvement plan priorities which relate to ECM/pupil well-being.				
Multi-agency practitioners are represented on the setting's leadership team.				
Multi-agency practitioners are represented on the setting's governing body/management board.				
Multi-agency practitioners are clear about the head teacher/head of centre's vision, aims and goals.				

Multi-agency practitioners are clear about the setting's accountability requirements and contribute robust evidence of the impact of their interventions to the SEF.			
Multi-agency practitioners report to the head or senior leadership team when required, in order to communicate their progress in improving pupils' ECM well-being outcomes.			
The head teacher/head of centre seeks service users' views and satisfaction levels with the services they have received from multi-agency practitioners, and compare this with the perceptions of the service providers.			
The effectiveness and quality of multi-agency partnerships are evaluated and reviewed within the setting, by the head of the setting.			

4a Communication and information sharing

Evidence descriptor	Emergent (early stages) – ✓ or ✗	Developing (in progress) – ✓ or ✗	Embedded (fully in place) – ✓ or ✗	Evaluative evidence/impact on pupils' ECM well-being outcomes
A common language is used by all multi-agency practitioners, which enables staff in the setting to understand terminology and acronyms used in reports and working practice.				
Clear protocols are in place for information sharing and using ContactPoint, and these are understood by all accessing it.				
Comprehensive, timely information is provided that enables multi-agency practitioners to deliver appropriate services and interventions to meet the needs of children/young people.				
Effective use is made of ICT to enable multi-agency practitioners to record, summarise, share and feedback information about interventions and work in progress.				
Confidentiality and agreements about access to confidential information are respected and understood among multi-agency practitioners, except when a child's safety and welfare are at risk.				

Information about the services being provided by multi-agency practitioners in the setting is available in a range of formats and languages for service users.				
Good effective channels of communication exist, which enable multi-agency practitioners to convey information, ideas, views among each other and with the relevant staff in the setting.				
Multi-agency practitioners listen to each others' views, and to those of service users, parents/carers and other staff.				
Multi-agency practitioners consult with children, young people and their parents/carers when making decisions about any changes to their provision.				
Multi-agency practitioners write reports that are jargon-free, understandable, factual, concise and which present objective judgements.				

Developing and Evaluating Multi-Agency Partnerships. A Practical Toolkit for Schools and Children's Centre Managers, Routledge Education © Rita Cheminais 2010.

5a Inter-professional relationships and roles

Evidence descriptor	Emergent (early stages) – ✓ or ✗	Developing (in progress) – ✓ or ✗	Embedded (fully in place) – ✓ or ✗	Evaluative evidence/impact on pupils' ECM well-being outcomes
Multi-agency practitioners' roles and responsibilities are clear, and staff in the setting know which services they can approach for further advice and support to help a child.				
The lead professional role is carried out effectively and efficiently.				
Multi-agency practitioners work collaboratively to discuss and solve problems, and to seek 'win–win' solutions relating to service provision for children and young people in the setting.				
Multi-agency practitioners share ideas and decision-making, and establish a true commitment to collaborative partnership working.				
Agreed targets and objectives for multi-agency working are shared across agencies and all practitioners are clear about their contribution to meeting these.				

Multi-agency practitioners follow through on any decisions that have been agreed in partnership with staff in the setting they are working in.				
Multi-agency practitioners are flexible and willing to make any changes to their working practice, or do things differently to improve outcomes for the children and young people they work with.				
Multi-agency practitioners continuously seek improvements in collaborative practice and better, more efficient ways of working.				
Early intervention is in evidence among multi-agency practitioners in order to remove barriers to learning and prevent problems occurring in the first place.				
Multi-agency practitioners are engaged in joint report writing, joint meetings, joint preparation and joint training which all help to strengthen collaborative partnership working.				

6a Team working

Evidence descriptor	Emergent (early stages) – ✓ or ✗	Developing (in progress) – ✓ or ✗	Embedded (fully in place) – ✓ or ✗	Evaluative evidence/impact on pupils' ECM well-being outcomes
Multi-agency practitioners operate within a 'no-blame' culture, where there is no buck-passing, and where there is a shared workload.				
Joint inter-professional training opportunities contribute to strengthening and further developing collaborative multi-agency teamwork within the setting.				
A 'can do' approach exists between multi-agency practitioners working within the setting's multi-disciplinary team.				
Multi-agency practitioners working within the setting form sustaining professional relationships, which help to clarify who is doing what and when, within the multi-disciplinary team.				
Multi-agency practitioners are clear about the expertise they bring to the multi-disciplinary team, and that of others.				

Time is made available for multi-agency team planning, team activities, and team developments, which help to build team capacity.				
Multi-agency practitioners from different services meet up together formally as a multi-professional team, at least once every half term to review provision and progress.				
Members of the multi-agency team within the setting have opportunities to share and disseminate good practice.				
The contributions that the multi-agency team make are valued by the staff in the setting, who appreciate the demands placed on partner agencies.				
Multi-agency teamwork/partnership working is recognised as a strength of the school by Ofsted, the LA, the SIP, parents/carers and the local community.				

7a Resources

Evidence descriptor	Emergent (early stages) – ✔ or ✗	Developing (in progress) – ✔ or ✗	Embedded (fully in place) – ✔ or ✗	Evaluative evidence/impact on pupils' ECM well-being outcomes
Multi-agency practitioners' share and pool resources/ budgets fairly for joint projects or initiatives.				
Multi-agency practitioners maintain records of expenditure and keep all receipts for any costs incurred in relation to their work with children and young people in the setting.				
Sufficient quality time is made available to enable multi-agency practitioners to attend relevant meetings, undertake CAF assessment work and write up written reports.				
Multi-agency practitioners demonstrate good value for money in relation to the services and interventions they deliver within the setting to children and young people.				
Multi-agency practitioners contribute to the setting's income generation by charging for some services/ activities.				

Statement				
Multi-agency practitioners have a dedicated budget for consumables such as stationery.				
Multi-agency practitioners have a budget for refreshments, drinks provided within their work area for visitors, parents/carers.				
Multi-agency practitioners follow the setting's procedures for booking the meeting room and contribute to any costs for printing minutes of meetings, briefing papers, reports for meetings, where appropriate.				
The setting's financial manager/bursar liaises with the multi-agency team regarding any budget issues, expenditure.				
Multi-agency practitioners keep the senior member of staff responsible for multi-agency working in the setting informed about any room maintenance issues or repairs required.				

8a Working with service users/clients

Evidence descriptor	Emergent (early stages) – ✓ or ✗	Developing (in progress) – ✓ or ✗	Embedded (fully in place) – ✓ or ✗	Evaluative evidence/impact on pupils' ECM well-being outcomes
Multi-agency practitioners in the setting take into account the preferences, feelings, wishes, needs and experiences of the children, young people and parents/carers they work with.				
Multi-agency practitioners listen to the views of children, young people, parents/carers and use these to inform their service provision and development.				
Multi-agency practitioners survey service users' views and satisfaction levels about the services provided, formally and annually.				
Multi-agency practitioners help children/young people they work with to make their own decisions and become independent, responsible individuals.				
Multi-agency practitioners make significant contributions to supporting children/young people during periods of transition or trauma in their lives.				

Multi-agency practitioners understand the needs of children/young people with special educational needs and disability, and adapt activities and provision accordingly to meet their needs.				
Multi-agency practitioners make valuable contributions to family learning, parent workshops, and to the EYFS or personal and social health education curriculum in the setting.				
Multi-agency practitioners ensure that the children/young people they are working with understand and know how they will be supporting them, and which ECM outcomes they will be working on.				
Multi-agency practitioners consult with parents/carers on what services they would find helpful in supporting their child and the family.				
Multi-agency practitioners ensure that parents/carers and other key stakeholders are kept informed about the impact of their work on improving their child's learning, well-being and personal development.				

9a Professional learning

Evidence descriptor	Emergent (early stages) – ✓ or ✗	Developing (in progress) – ✓ or ✗	Embedded (fully in place) – ✓ or ✗	Evaluative evidence/impact on pupils' ECM well-being outcomes
Multi-agency practitioners are willing to learn from each other and share experiences, knowledge and skills across services.				
There are effective staff support arrangements for multi-agency practitioners working within the setting.				
Multi-agency practitioners are engaged in joint inter-professional training, INSET sessions with staff in the setting.				
Opportunities are available for early-years practitioners, teaching and learning support staff to undertake work shadowing and observation of different multi-agency practitioners at work, and vice versa.				
A range of approaches are available for multi-agency practitioners continuing professional development, e.g. face-to-face training, e-learning, distance learning; mentoring and coaching; observation.				
Multi-agency practitioners continuously seek ways to improve their working practice within the setting.				

Opportunities are provided for multi-agency practitioners to work and learn together on joint projects/initiatives to innovate and develop best-practice in joint collaborative working.			
Multi-agency practitioners are given feedback on their service delivery and impact as part of the setting's improvement and self-evaluation processes.			
Multi-agency practitioners are given opportunities to network with other practitioners from their service, enabling the dissemination and exchange of best practice to occur.			
Multi-agency practitioners maintain a portfolio of professional learning and development which records significant achievements in working with children and young people in the setting.			

Every evidence descriptor for each of the nine multi-agency working aspects should be embedded by the end of the self-evaluation process, particularly for those education settings and services who wish to achieve an award. There is a good level of rigour, ambition and challenge in the entire process. The nine completed multi-agency self-evaluation grids need to be included in the portfolio of evidence.

It is good practice, but not compulsory, for education settings and services to moderate their multi-agency working judgements within their own setting or service, as well as across a range of other similar settings or services within an LA area.

Undertaking the audit for multi-agency working

The audit, using the self-evaluation grids, needs to be undertaken once a working party or task group has been formed. This group should comprise of nine appropriate individuals who will each take responsibility for auditing one of the nine aspects.

The audit will entail each member of the working party indicating on the relevant self-evaluation grid whether each of the ten elements is emergent, developing or embedded. The timescale for the completion of the initial audit is 2–3 weeks. Once the audit has been completed, the working party or task group should meet together to review and discuss the findings. The audit will help to identify any existing gaps in each of the nine aspects of multi-agency working. Actions and activities for addressing the elements that require further improvement to advance them to the embedded level will also be agreed. A summary of findings from the audit will be written up as a report by the senior member of staff overseeing the entire self-evaluation process. This audit report needs to be included in the multi-agency portfolio of evidence.

The advantages of undertaking a multi-agency audit

The three main advantages of undertaking an audit of multi-agency working are:

- it helps to benchmark current practice against the evidence descriptors;

- it helps to identify strengths and areas for further development in multi-agency working;
- it enables shared ownership and distributed leadership for multi-agency working to take place across an education setting or service.

Producing a multi-agency action plan

The senior member of staff responsible for overseeing the multi-agency self-evaluation process will need to produce the multi-agency action plan. A template for the action plan can be downloaded from the Routledge Education website, and is also provided here.

The action plan will:
- identify the key priorities for further action;
- identify the activities/action that needs to take place to meet the priorities;
- identify the lead person responsible for undertaking and monitoring the actions and activities;
- identify a realistic timescale for the actions and activities to be undertaken;
- identify any necessary resources to meet the priorities, e.g. time;
- specify the expected success criteria or performance measures for each priority/activity.

Each person identified as being responsible for a priority and its activities will also take responsibility for monitoring and reviewing the ongoing progress. The working party will need to meet at least once every half term to report back collectively to the senior member of staff on the progress made. Most action plans cover a period of twelve months, but this may vary according to the context the education setting or service is working within.

Support and consultancy for those seeking an award

Those education settings or services who wish to achieve an award for their multi-agency working can choose one of the three packages of support and consultancy available from Every Child Matters (ECM) Solutions:

Table 2.1 Action plan template for multi-agency working 20____ to 20____

Multi-agency aspect	Actions/activities	Lead person	Resources	Timescale (start and completion date)	Monitoring (who, when, how)	Success criteria/performance Indicators
1. Policy, procedures and legal requirements						
2. The working environment						
3. Leadership and management						
4. Communication and information sharing						
5. Inter-professional relationships and roles						
6. Team working						
7. Resources						
8. Working with service users and clients						
9. Professional learning						

GOLD

This offers the higher level of support and consultancy, which includes:

- an initial visit from the Every Child Matters (ECM) Solutions consultant;
- the delivery of in-service education and training (INSET) to introduce the award process to stakeholders;
- access to ongoing telephone and email support and consultancy;
- an interim visit to review progress towards gathering evidence;
- an on-site half-day assessment with collection of the portfolio;
- a full written report of the outcomes of the assessment;
- a glass plaque, a framed certificate and a digital logo.

SILVER

This offers a reduced level of support and consultancy. It includes:

- access to ongoing telephone and email support and consultancy;
- an interim visit to review progress towards gathering evidence;
- an on-site half-day assessment with collection of the portfolio;
- a full written report of the outcomes of assessment;
- a glass plaque, a framed certificate and a digital logo.

BRONZE

This package offers the minimum level of consultancy and support. It includes:

- access to telephone and email support and consultancy when required;
- an on-site half-day assessment with collection of the portfolio;
- a full written report of the outcomes of assessment;
- a glass plaque, a framed certificate and a digital logo.

Additional consultancy and support can be purchased on a pay-as-you-go basis for any of the three packages. Each package requires a contract of agreement to be signed by both parties and an initial part-payment (half the cost of the total package) to be made at the start of the award process.

3

Compiling a multi-agency portfolio of evidence

The aim of the portfolio of evidence

The portfolio of evidence is an essential stage in the multi-agency self-evaluation process. The aim in compiling the portfolio is to gather together a range of high-quality information and telling evidence in one or two volumes on all the aspects of multi-agency working.

The portfolio enables the education setting or service to showcase their achievements and experiences in multi-agency working. The portfolio of evidence is a living document which illustrates the journey taken in working towards meeting each of the nine multi-agency working aspects.

Compiling the portfolio of evidence helps to inform a range of stakeholders, such as the School Improvement Partner (SIP), the Ofsted inspector, the LA and the external assessor about the activities and actions undertaken, in order to further develop and improve collaborative, integrated multi-agency working within an education setting.

Using the portfolio of evidence checklists and evidence sheets

The points listed below will help those taking responsibility for each of the nine aspects of multi-agency working to gather the appropriate evidence. The checklists are designed to act as quick prompts to ensure all essential evidence has been considered. The evidence sheets provide examples of the types of evidence to collect in order to meet the ten evidence descriptors for each multi-agency aspect.

- Work through the checklist prompts sequentially.
- Ensure that evidence from other awards, or in the SEF, are cross-referenced where appropriate on each evidence sheet.
- Other appropriate evidence not listed in the good practice examples on the evidence sheets can be added.
- Good practice examples can be highlighted if included in the portfolio, in addition to listing them in the first section on the evidence sheets.
- Evidence should be dated as it is put into the portfolio.
- All evidence included in the portfolio must be an accurate representation of the progress made throughout the self-evaluation process.
- A contents page should be included at the front of the portfolio.
- The action plan should be put at the front of the portfolio of evidence, along with the completed audit and the report of findings from the audit.
- A divider should be used for each of the nine aspects included in the portfolio, with the completed self-evaluation sheet, the portfolio checklist and the completed portfolio of evidence sheet placed at the front of each section.
- Include any examples of the reflection surveys, which gather the views of those leading and participating in the self-evaluation process, at the end of the portfolio.
- Ensure the portfolio is well organised and easy to navigate. Ideally, is should be no more than two volumes.

The format of evidence to collect for the multi-agency portfolio

All evidence for the portfolio does not have to be in a written format. Any of the following formats are acceptable:
- photographs
- DVDs/CDs
- diary room videos
- audio recordings with transcripts
- observational accounts
- documentary evidence, as listed in the good practice examples, but which can include:

- minutes of significant relevant meetings
- newsletters
- surveys, questionnaires and their findings
- any promotional information
- media articles
- reports and briefing papers
- case studies, cameos of real success stories in multi-agency working
- extracts from the education setting's or service's website
- relevant sections from the SEF and improvement plan
- statistical data that demonstrates improvement in well-being outcomes
- mission statements, prospectuses, profiles, key policies.

The portfolio checklists and the portfolio evidence sheets are featured in this chapter. They are also available to download at: www. routledge.com/education.

Portfolio checklist for policy, procedures and legal requirements

- The senior member of staff responsible for overseeing the multi-agency self-evaluation process has seen all multi-agency practitioners CRB certificates.
- Evidence exists of the most recent safeguarding and health and safety training attended by multi-agency practitioners working in the setting.
- Service level agreements and contracts have been signed by both parties.
- Consistent procedures and proformas are used by all multi-agency practitioners for reports and recording information within the setting.
- There is a named person within the education setting responsible for commissioning and brokering multi-agency services within the setting.
- Clear procedures exist for engaging with the local Children's Trust.

Developing and Evaluating Multi-Agency Partnerships. A Practical Toolkit for Schools and Children's Centre Managers, Routledge Education © Rita Cheminais 2010.

Portfolio checklist for the working environment

- The physical working environment where multi-agency practitioners work within the education setting is pleasant, well maintained, safe and healthy.
- Attractive, interesting and informative displays related to multi-agency working are evident in the base/area within the education setting.
- There is a telephone/intercom system in the working area for emergencies.
- Appropriate levels of sound-proofing exist in the smaller rooms/offices used for counselling work.
- Where possible, there is an external entrance to the base or multi-agency working area so parents/carers/community members can enter discreetly.
- Furniture in the multi-agency working area is comfortable and at the appropriate height, particularly for wheelchair users.
- The multi-agency working area has secure storage facilities.
- Any specialist or electrical equipment used by multi-agency practitioners within the base or working area has been safety checked and is in good working order.

Portfolio checklist for leadership and management

- There is a nominated member of the governing body or management board responsible for multi-agency working in the education setting.
- The working party/task group within the setting are taking full leadership responsibility for gathering evidence and monitoring and reporting progress to the senior member of staff responsible for overseeing the multi-agency process.
- There is a strategic improvement plan in place which identifies those responsible for undertaking the activities and actions to improve aspects of multi-agency working.
- The head teacher of the setting knows which multi-agency practitioners are working with specifically targeted children and young people, and the nature of the service provision being delivered.

Developing and Evaluating Multi-Agency Partnerships. A Practical Toolkit for Schools and Children's Centre Managers, Routledge Education © Rita Cheminais 2010.

- There is a lead member of the multi-agency team within the setting who is responsible for referring any issues or concerns to the designated senior member of staff who oversees multi-agency working.
- The head teacher of the setting will challenge poor or ineffective multi-agency provision being delivered to children and young people.

Portfolio checklist for communication and information sharing

- There is a guide for staff within the education setting. This defines the common terminology and the acronyms used by multi-agency practitioners.
- The senior member of staff responsible for overseeing multi-agency working within the education setting has ensured that access to relevant databases and ContactPoint are available to multi-agency practitioners on-site.
- There is a directory of local services for service users/staff which is available online and in hard copy within the education setting.
- The dates and times when multi-agency services are available within the education setting are publicised to service users, staff and parents/carers.
- The senior member of staff responsible for overseeing multi-agency working within the education setting is approachable and accessible to multi-agency practitioners.
- Information about the nature of services available from multi-agency practitioners within the education setting is provided in a range of alternative formats and languages.

Portfolio checklist for inter-professional relationships and roles

- The senior member of staff responsible for multi-agency working within the education setting has ensured all staff/stakeholders know the roles and responsibilities of all the multi-agency practitioners working with children and young people.

- Although the Lead Professional for a child/young person may change over time, everyone within the education setting is clear about their role.

- Multi-agency practitioners are encouraged to participate in joint problem-solving and joint decision-making with other stakeholders within the education setting.

- Joint inter-professional working is encouraged and promoted between multi-agency practitioners and staff within the education setting.

- Multi-agency practitioners are given opportunities to express their views and opinions, which are listened to by those within the education setting.

- It is accepted that there may be occasions when integrated multi-agency working may not meet a child's or young person's needs, and may not be the appropriate solution.

Portfolio checklist for team working

- All staff within the education setting know which practitioners are in the multi-agency team.

- The multi-agency team's role has been clarified with staff in the education setting. For example, what the TAC role and purpose is.

- Staff within the education setting know when and how to access the advice and support of the multi-agency team.

- Staff briefings and staff meetings within the education setting acknowledge the good work undertaken by the multi-agency team.

- Any changes in the operation or membership of the multi-agency team within the education setting are made clear to staff and service users.

- The value-added that the multi-agency team contributes to the work of the education setting is recorded in the SEF.

Developing and Evaluating Multi-Agency Partnerships. A Practical Toolkit for Schools and Children's Centre Managers, Routledge Education © Rita Cheminais 2010.

Portfolio checklist for resources

- There is an allocated budget available for multi-agency joint initiatives and projects within the education setting which help to improve ECM outcomes.
- The senior member of staff responsible for multi-agency working within the setting monitors the budget and expenditure for multi-agency work.
- Time to free-up multi-agency practitioners to attend meetings, case conferences or courses are accounted for in the setting of staff cover costs.
- Monthly or quarterly statements of the charges for room hire, phone bills and photocopying costs incurred by multi-agency practitioners working in the setting are sent to their service managers.
- The multi-agency team are introduced to the education setting's bursar or finance officer, who has provides them with guidance on keeping records of all expenses incurred as part of their work.
- There is a report given each term at the governor's or management board's finance committee meeting, relating to multi-agency expenditure and value-for-money outcomes.

Portfolio checklist for working with service users/clients

- Children and young people are given every opportunity to voice their views about the multi-agency services they receive in the setting.
- Parents/carers know who the point of contact is within the education setting and to whom they can express any concerns or views about multi-agency services.
- Parents/carers know how and where to access the local Parent Partnership Service to discuss any issues about multi-agency service provision within the education setting.
- Newsletters to parents/carers and information on the education setting's website are utilised to promote the positive benefits and outcomes of having multi-agency services available in the education setting.

- Children and/or young people within the education setting, accessing multi-agency services, have a key adult to whom they can relate any views about the services they receive.
- There is a suggestion box available within the education setting where service users can post comments anonymously about multi-agency services they have accessed.

Portfolio checklist for professional learning

- Multi-agency practitioners have been consulted about their professional development needs to enable them to work more effectively in the setting.
- All new practitioners joining the multi-agency team receive an induction programme, which is designed to support them during their first year of working within the education setting.
- Multi-agency practitioners are given the opportunity to contribute to the education settings annual continuing professional development (CPD) programme.
- Multi-agency practitioners know they can have an annual professional review meeting within the education setting.
- Multi-agency practitioners are invited to make contributions to any local learning network or cluster group meetings in order to share good practice.
- Multi-agency practitioners know they need to let the CPD coordinator in the setting know which local, regional or national conferences and training courses they have applied to attend throughout the year.

1c Portfolio of evidence sheet for policy, procedures and legal requirements

Key evidence collected	Evidence location and links to other awards and the SEF	Good-practice examples of evidence
		Policies for partnership working and multi-agency working.
		Examples of service level agreements, multi-agency partnership agreement.
		Outlines of multi-agency services procedures for alerts, referral, assessment, ceasing provision or closing a case.
		Procedures and examples for brokering and commissioning services, and partnership working with the local Children's Trust.
		Examples of any CAF guidance produced by services to support the holistic assessment process.
		Templates used for record keeping
		Policies for equal opportunities, health and safety, safeguarding, child protection or whistle blowing that multi-agency practitioners follow within the setting.
		Photographic evidence of any displays/notices which illustrate procedures, safety requirements in the multi-agency working area/base.
		Minutes from any multi-agency operational meetings that make reference to any policy, procedures or legal requirements linked to their work in the setting.
		Evidence and dated records of all multi-agency CRB certificates.

2c Portfolio of evidence sheet for the working environment

Key evidence collected	Evidence location and links to other awards and the SEF	Good-practice examples of evidence
		Documentary evidence such as responses from multi-agency practitioners in questionnaires or surveys as to how welcome they feel in the setting.
		Photographic evidence of the multi-agency working area within the education setting, which indicates rooms available and facilities.
		Records of clerical tasks and administrative support multi-agency practitioners receive from the education setting's administrative team.
		Example of a multi-agency practitioner's identity badge worn in the education setting.
		Any records of multi-agency practitioners participating in any activities or events run by the education setting.
		Records of maintenance and repairs carried out for the multi-agency working area.
		Views of multi-agency practitioners about the quality and fitness for purpose of their working environment within the education setting.

Photographic evidence of health and safety notices within the multi-agency practitioners working area within the setting.	Records of specialist equipment safety checks and the maintenance of any computer hardware which are used by multi-agency practitioners within the setting.	Evidence of safety precautions for emergencies within the multi-agency working area, e.g. telephone, concealed panic buttons, personal alarms for multi-agency workers.	

Developing and Evaluating Multi-Agency Partnerships. A Practical Toolkit for Schools and Children's Centre Managers, Routledge Education © Rita Cheminais 2010.

3c Portfolio of evidence sheet for leadership and management

Key evidence collected	Evidence location and links to other awards and the SEF	Good-practice examples of evidence
		Minutes from staff meetings and briefings within the education setting that make reference to the multi-agency team/workers.
		Evidence from reports/minutes of the involvement of multi-agency practitioners in the setting's improvement planning process.
		List of members on the education setting's senior leadership team which indicates any multi-agency representatives.
		List of members on the governing body or management board of the setting, and which are multi-agency representatives.
		Evidence of multi-agency practitioners' involvement in the education settings self-evaluation process, e.g. relevant SEF extracts.
		Minutes of meetings and progress reports prepared by multi-agency practitioners for the education settings SLT.
		Reports and summaries from governing body or management board meetings on the ongoing work and interventions of the multi-agency team.

Celebrations and showcase events which acknowledge the work of the multi-agency practitioners within the setting.	Annual report of the head of the education setting which indicates the evidence and impact of multi-agency service provision within the setting.	A list of changes made which have helped to improve multi-agency service provision within the setting.

4c Portfolio of evidence sheet for communication and information sharing

Key evidence collected	Evidence location and links to other awards and the SEF	Good-practice examples of evidence
		Samples of a range of information leaflets, brochures, CD/DVD, website links, audio tapes, describing the work of the multi-agency services in the education setting.
		Written policy and procedures about confidentiality, and data protection, relevant to multi-agency practitioners working in the education setting.
		Evidence from significant consultation exercises with service users as to how useful they found the information about the services provided.
		Examples of clear signage utilised within the education setting and the multi-agency working area to indicate the base's location.
		Samples of some non-confidential information that is shared and utilised among multi-agency practitioners and relevant staff in the education setting.
		An example of the guidance used to support staff and multi-agency practitioners in utilising ContactPoint.
		Photographic evidence of any information boards or electronic visual displays about the multi-agency services provided in the education setting.

	Records of when and who is accessing any databases containing information about children and young people, ContactPoint and CAF online.	A record of the quality time made available for multi-agency practitioners and staff to share and disseminate information.	A sample of reports from multi-agency practitioners which are anonymous and non-confidential.

5c Portfolio of evidence sheet for inter-professional relationships and roles

Key evidence collected	Evidence location and links to other awards and the SEF	Good-practice examples of evidence
		Job descriptions for multi-agency practitioners.
		Evaluations and outcomes from joint inter-professional training sessions.
		Cameos, written accounts of shared multi-agency problem solving.
		Examples of successful initiatives, joint projects that have helped to promote and further develop inter-professional working between multi-agency practitioners and staff in the education setting.
		A list that summarises any significant shared decisions made as a result of inter-professional collaboration.
		Examples of agreed targets, objectives, goals relating to inter-professional working within the setting.
		Case studies, cameos of examples where inter-professional roles have had to be changed or modified in order to meet the needs of particular service users/children.

Minutes from any significant meetings that illustrate or describe inter-professional expectations from their work within the education setting.	Case studies or cameos which illustrate early intervention taking place through inter-professional working.	Any photographic, CD/DVD evidence of inter-professional working in action.

6c Portfolio of evidence sheet for team working

Key evidence collected	Evidence location and links to other awards and the SEF	Good-practice examples of evidence
		Evaluations from any joint training events attended by multi-agency team members, which demonstrate positive outcomes for joint working.
		Case studies which demonstrate how the multi-agency team have resolved or overcome any difficult issues.
		Professional profiles of members of the multi-agency team which illustrate the breadth of experience, skills and length of time they have been working within the education setting/LA.
		Multi-agency workers' timetables and case loads which illustrate the extent of their work within the education setting.
		Photographs with the names and role of all members in the multi-agency team which are displayed in the main entrance of the setting and/or outside the multi-agency working area.
		Calendars and diary extracts which show how time has been allocated to the multi-agency team for planning, meetings, joint project work and training.
		Samples of minutes from multi-agency team meetings.

Developing and Evaluating Multi-Agency Partnerships. A Practical Toolkit for Schools and Children's Centre Managers, Routledge Education © Rita Cheminais 2010.

A list of all the expertise, skills and knowledge shared between multi-agency team members and with staff in the education setting.	Cameos or snapshots from case studies which demonstrate the extra efforts, e.g. through the TAC approach, that multi-agency practitioners have taken.	Extracts from any Ofsted, SIP or LA reports that highlight or mention good and outstanding practice in multi-agency team working.

Developing and Evaluating Multi-Agency Partnerships. A Practical Toolkit for Schools and Children's Centre Managers, Routledge Education © Rita Cheminais 2010.

7c Portfolio of evidence sheet for resources

Key evidence collected	Evidence location and links to other awards and the SEF	Good-practice examples of evidence
		Examples of any pooled or shared multi-agency budgets for joint work with a report on outcomes.
		Sample pages of monthly records of multi-agency practitioners' expenditure within the setting for consumables and refreshments.
		A couple of examples of reports which demonstrate best value outcomes in return for expenditure on multi-agency service provision.
		Records of multi-agency staff cover costs when any practitioners are attending meetings or courses.
		Example of accounts for any income generated by multi-agency practitioners offering services within the setting, and a report on how this money was utilised.
		An annual report from the setting's bursar or finance office relating to expenditure on multi-agency work and whether it has provided good value for money.
		Statement or balance sheet indicating maintenance costs for the facilities used by multi-agency practitioners within the setting over one year.

Annual report on the pros and cons of providing the multi-agency team within the setting with clerical and administrative support.	Sample of briefing papers, minutes and reports prepared for multi-agency meetings within the setting, which are not confidential.	Feedback from service users on the value for money of accessing any chargeable or free multi-agency services within the setting.

8c Portfolio of evidence sheet for working with service users/clients

Key evidence collected	Evidence location and links to other awards and the SEF	Good-practice examples of evidence
		Minutes from school council meetings, any children and young people's forums; comments and feedback from parents/carers.
		Evidence from service users' surveys or discussions on how their views have led to changes or improvements in the multi-agency services offered within the setting.
		Statistical data which illustrates service users attendance and satisfaction levels with multi-agency services available within the setting, and analysis to identify any gaps or trends in service provision.
		Cameos or case studies which illustrate the progress made by children or young people as a result of receiving multi-agency service provision.
		Evidence of multi-agency work undertaken to support children or young people with transition in their lives, e.g. moving to the next key stage or year group in the education setting.
		The setting's accessibility plan to indicate any adaptations made by multi-agency practitioners within the setting to enable children and young people with physical disabilities or sensory impairments to access services.

	Programmes outlining parent workshops, family learning activities, EYFS or personal and social health curriculum contributions delivered by multi-agency practitioners working within the setting.	Examples of any individual children plans, audio recordings and/or transcripts which indicate how their ECM well-being outcomes have been improved as a result of multi-agency working.	Findings from any service users' consultations.	Examples of multi-agency review meeting reports.

Developing and Evaluating Multi-Agency Partnerships. A Practical Toolkit for Schools and Children's Centre Managers, Routledge Education © Rita Cheminais 2010.

9c Portfolio of evidence sheet for professional learning

Key evidence collected	Evidence location and links to other awards and the SEF	Good-practice examples of evidence
		Sample of any INSET programmes within the setting which feature any joint inter-professional training activities or sessions.
		Samples from multi-agency practitioners professional development portfolios.
		Evaluations on the impact of any training sessions delivered by multi-agency staff within the setting, which have led to improvements in staff collaborative working.
		Examples of any PowerPoint presentations focusing on multi-agency working within the setting.
		Samples of feedback from multi-agency practitioners on any INSET training or courses they have attended which have helped to support their work within the setting.
		Examples of minutes from meetings which relate to multi-agency practitioners professional development.
		Cameos or snapshots of successful multi-agency professional learning outcomes.

		Samples of any training materials used or accessed by staff within the setting or by multi-agency practitioners, which promote professional learning.	Written reports from any work shadowing experiences.	Evidence from the setting's website, or from local cluster group or network meetings that disseminate the good practice in multi-agency professional learning.

4

Monitoring, evaluating and assessing progress in multi-agency working

Monitoring multi-agency working

Monitoring is the ongoing process of tracking the progress being made towards meeting all ten elements for each of the nine aspects of multi-agency working, which make up the self-evaluation process. The senior member of staff responsible for overseeing the entire multi-agency self-evaluation process within the education setting is accountable to the head teacher and the governing body or management board. He or she is expected to provide them with at least one update per term on the progress being made towards meeting all nine multi-agency working aspects.

The nine people in the working party, each responsible for gathering evidence for meeting the ten elements of their aspect of multi-agency working, should meet formally with the senior member of staff leading the process, each half term, to report back on progress made.

The evidence reported back by the members of the working party or task group is then summarised and written up by the senior member of staff leading the multi-agency self-evaluation process, as part of the interim review reports, which are placed in the portfolio of evidence. These summary reports can be bullet-point progress lists, cross-referenced to the relevant actions and activities on the action plan. Box 4.1 provides a model template for recording progress for the periodic monitoring of each of the nine aspects of multi-agency working.

Box 4.1 Model template for monitoring interim progress in multi-agency working

Multi-agency aspect: _____

Lead person: _____ Date: _____

1. Which elements of the multi-agency aspect have been covered this term?

2. What progress has been made in meeting the elements for the aspect?

3. What key evidence for the elements covered during this period has been recorded on the portfolio of evidence sheet?

4. Which, if any, of the elements were the most challenging to gather evidence for?

5. Which, if any, of the elements covered this term require further action?

6. Which three elements of the multi-agency aspect will be monitored next term?

7. Are there any other comments you wish to make about the elements monitored this term?

Developing and Evaluating Multi-Agency Partnerships. A Practical Toolkit for Schools and Children's Centre Managers, Routledge Education © Rita Cheminais 2010.

Evaluating and assessing progress in the multi-agency self-evaluation process

Evaluation entails judging the effectiveness, strengths and weaknesses of the multi-agency self-evaluation process in order to interpret how well things are going. It is important that the senior member of staff responsible for leading and overseeing the entire multi-agency self-evaluation process evaluates the overall experience. He or she needs to gather the views of those taking responsibility for each of the nine aspects of multi-agency working, using the model survey. Box 4.2, shown here and also downloadable from the Routledge Education website, provides a suitable survey.

Box 4.2 Model survey for those leading on an aspect of multi-agency working

---

Multi-agency aspect: _____

Job title: _____

Please answer the following questions as fully as possible. Return your completed survey to the deputy head teacher within one week of completion.

1. What have been the main advantages of monitoring an aspect of multi-agency working?

2. What, if any, barriers existed to collecting evidence for your aspect of multi-agency working?

3. What strengths and good practice have you identified in relation to your aspect of multi-agency working?

4. Which elements of multi-agency working required further action or developments in relation to your aspect?

---

5. What has been the greatest achievement or improvement made in relation to your aspect of multi-agency working?

6. How could the multi-agency self-evaluation process be further improved?

7. What challenges, if any, did you face in engaging with the multi-agency self-evaluation process?

8. What have you gained professionally from being part of the multi-agency self-evaluation process?

9. What evidence was the most difficult to collect for your multi-agency aspect?

10. Do you consider the multi-agency self-evaluation process to be manageable?

11. Are there any further comments you wish to make about the multi-agency self-evaluation process?

This evidence needs to be written up as a report and included at the end of the multi-agency portfolio of evidence. Boxes 4.3 and 4.4 provide model stakeholder surveys to use.

Box 4.3 Model survey for multi-agency practitioners in the school

Please complete the following survey and return to the Head of Partnerships.

Please circle YES or NO for each question

Service: _____   Date completed: _____

1. Are you familiar with all relevant policies, procedures and legal requirements that influence your work with children in school?
YES ☐   NO ☐
If NO, which policy, procedure or legal requirement do you need to know?

2. Have you found your working environment in the setting to be suitable?
YES ☐   NO ☐
If NO, please indicate what would improve your working environment.

3. Do you consider the multi-agency team you work in within the setting to be well led, managed and organised?
YES ☐   NO ☐
If NO, what would improve the leadership and management of the team?

4. Do you consider there is good communication and information sharing taking place between multi-agency practitioners and staff in the setting?
YES ☐   NO ☐
If NO, what would improve communication and information sharing?

5. Are the roles and responsibilities of all practitioners in the multi-agency team clear?
YES ☐   NO ☐
If NO, which roles and responsibilities have been unclear?

6. If you have worked as a Lead Professional or in a Team Around the Child in school, have you felt well supported by other colleagues in the team?
YES ☐   NO ☐
If NO, what would make working in these roles more effective?

7. Have resources been sufficient for multi-agency working in the setting?
   YES ☐   NO ☐
   If NO, what further resources would you welcome?

8. Have you found working with service users a positive experience?
   YES ☐   NO ☐
   If NO, why not, and what would help to form more productive relationships?

9. Have you found the CPD courses attended this year helpful to your role?
   YES ☐   NO ☐
   If NO, which CPD would you value attending this year?

10. Please make any further comments about multi-agency working in the setting.

Thank you for completing this survey.

Box 4.4 Model survey for service users/ clients

Please complete this survey and return to the Head of Partnerships.

Tick one box for each question.

Are you a parent/carer? ☐   Are you a pupil in the school/setting? ☐

1. Which service(s) have you used or received this year in the school/setting?

   Health ☐   Social Care ☐   Education Welfare ☐   Connexions ☐
   Other – please state:

2. Have the service(s) been helpful to you and offered good support and advice?
   YES ☐   NO ☐
   If NO, please state why, and what would make the service(s) better for you.

3. Have you found the room(s) where the services are delivered suitable?
   YES ☐   NO ☐
   If NO, please state why, and what would make the room better.

4. Were you always made to feel welcome by service workers?
   YES ☐   NO ☐
   If NO, please state why, and what might make you feel more welcome.

5. Were your views listened to by the multi-agency staff working with you?
   YES ☐   NO ☐
   If NO, please state what would help these workers listen to your views.

6. Did you have a chance to give your opinions about the service(s) received?
   YES ☐   NO ☐
   If NO, why not? If YES, did it help to improve the service(s) you receive?

7. Were you clear about the roles of all the staff from different services working with you in school?
   YES ☐   NO ☐
   If NO, what would help to make service staff roles clearer to you?

8. Did all multi-agency staff working with you keep you informed about your progress, or any changes to be made in service provision?
   YES ☐   NO ☐
   If NO, what would improve keeping you informed about service provision and your progress better?

9. What else would you like to comment about below, in relation to the multi-agency services you have received within the school/setting this year?

Thank you for completing this survey.

The education setting needs to demonstrate value-added progress in relation to the nine aspects of multi-agency working, particularly in relation to improving children and young people's well-being. This entire self-evaluation process enables senior leaders in the education

Developing and Evaluating Multi-Agency Partnerships. A Practical Toolkit for Schools and Children's Centre Managers, Routledge Education © Rita Cheminais 2010.

setting to demonstrate the effectiveness of their multi-agency working, which can be shared with external professionals such as the SIP, Ofsted inspectors and LA officers.

The external assessment for those settings seeking an award

Those education settings that have signed an agreement to obtain an award in recognition for their good practice in multi-agency working will need to engage in a half-day on-site assessment, undertaken by the external assessor from Every Child Matters (ECM) Solutions. The programme for the half-day assessment is agreed between the assessor and the head teacher of the setting. An example of a half-day external assessment is illustrated below:

8.30–8.40	Arrival of the external assessor.
8.40–9.20	Meeting with the head teacher, Chair of Governors/Management Board and the senior lead member of staff overseeing the process.
9.30–10.00	Observation of multi-agency provision in practice.
10.00–10.30	Focused discussion with the multi-agency practitioners observed.
10.30–11.00	Meeting with a sample of service users to gather views on multi-agency provision available within the setting.
11.00–11.30	Meeting with those leading on an aspect of multi-agency working.
11.30–12.00	Meeting with education staff supporting multi-agency working, e.g. bursar, administrative assistant, site manager.
12.00–12.50	Lunch with children and observation of any lunchtime multi-agency activities.
13.00–13.30	Verbal feedback on observations from half day assessment to the head teacher and the senior member of staff leading multi-agency working.
13.35	Departure of the assessor with the portfolio of evidence.

What the education setting receives as an outcome of external assessment

Following the half-day on-site assessment, the external assessor will take the multi-agency portfolio of evidence away for assessment. The assessor will produce a full written report of findings from the on-site assessment and the portfolio of evidence. This report will be sent to the education setting within four weeks from the date of the on-site assessment.

The external assessor will agree a date for the presentation of the multi-agency award plaque and framed certificate at the education setting. The final payment will be made by the education setting on achieving the award.

A digital logo for achieving the multi-agency award will be sent to the education setting to use on their stationery.

> The multi-agency award is valid for three years. This multi-agency award is only valid if it comes from Every Child Matters (ECM) Solutions. A setting can apply to be re-assessed, and if successful in the re-assessment, they can renew their award for a further three years.

5

Achievements and outcomes of engaging with the multi-agency self-evaluation process

The achievements from engaging with the multi-agency self-evaluation process

The achievements are many for those schools, children's centres, services and practitioners engaging with the multi-agency self-evaluation/award process. Table 5.1 provides a useful summary of the main achievements.

Those schools, children's centres and services systematically gathering evidence for each of the nine multi-agency aspects will experience a great sense of achievement, in view of the rigour and robustness of the self-evaluation process.

Leaders of schools will find that by engaging with the multi-agency self-evaluation process they will gain valuable knowledge and skills relevant to the National Standards for School Leadership in the areas of *Leading People* and *Leading in the Community*, both of which cover aspects of multi-agency working. Similarly, heads of children's centres will also gain the necessary skills relating to multi-agency partnership working that feature in the National Standards for Leaders of Sure Start Children's Centres', *Building and Strengthening Teams*.

The multi-agency self-evaluation process described in this book will enable those working in children's services, who deliver direct support and interventions to children and young people in schools

Table 5.1 Achievements for schools and children's workforce practitioners engaging with the multi-agency self-evaluation process

Achievements for multi-agency practitioners	Achievements for schools and children's centres
• Increases the confidence of multi-agency practitioners through the ongoing robust evidence-gathering process, in knowing that they have met the common core of skills and knowledge for multi-agency working • Enhances and extends multi-agency practitioners' professional learning • Sharpens multi-agency practitioners' focus on the impact of their services/interventions in improving outcomes for children and young people • Leads to more sustainable multi-disciplinary partnership working • Increases the self-esteem, self-confidence and motivation of multi-agency practitioners engaging with the self-evaluation/award process	• Efficient and effective multi-agency teamwork leads to better ECM outcomes for children and young people in the school/children's centre • Ensures teaching and support staff meet the requirements of the Professional Standards for Teachers and the National Occupational Standards for Supporting Teaching and Learning, in the aspect of working with other colleagues/practitioners • A holistic approach to meeting the needs of the whole child by working in partnership with other agencies becomes embedded as part of every day practice • Offers the opportunity to gain recognition – beyond Ofsted – for their good practice in multi-agency working • Helps to raise the profile of multi-agency partnership working within the school/children's centre, and beyond, in the wider community

and children's centres, to provide high-quality integrated services that will meet the government's expectations and legal requirements.

The Every Child Matters (ECM) Solutions website will publicise and disseminate the good practice in multi-agency working, as schools, children's centres, services and other education settings achieve the multi-agency award.

The outcomes of engaging with the multi-agency self-evaluation process

As a result of engaging with this multi-agency self-evaluation process, schools, children's centres and other education settings will achieve the following outcomes:

- greater clarity of purpose in working with a diverse range of multi-agency services and organisations;
- a clearer common understanding of the professional language used across different multi-agency disciplines;
- improved two-way communication between the setting and the various agencies;
- strengthened engagement and involvement of multi-agency practitioners and professionals in whole-school improvement planning and self-evaluation processes;
- fostered inter-professional learning across agencies and the education setting/children's centre;
- promoted shared ownership and collective responsibility for improving the ECM outcomes for children and young people within the learning community;
- improved integrated multi-agency working within the education setting or children's centre;
- break down of existing organisational and traditional cross-service/agency barriers in order to promote improved collaborative multi-agency partnerships.

Those settings or services meeting all nine aspects of multi-agency working at the embedded level will have high-quality evidence to present to the LA, Ofsted inspectors and the SIP. SIPs will want to know:

- How well does the school perform in relation to improving pupils' well-being as a result of multi-agency partnership working?
- What are the strengths of multi-agency partnership working within the school?
- What are the areas for further development or improvement in multi-agency partnership working?
- What is the pupil level attainment and ECM well-being data indicating, as a result of multi-agency interventions?
- Are there any surprises in what the data is telling you?
- Are there any gaps in multi-agency provision or ECM outcomes for particular groups of pupils?
- If there are gaps in provision and outcomes, how will these be addressed?

- Have the priorities/activities related to multi-agency working on the school improvement plan been met?
- What have been the views of service users about the multi-agency services they have accessed at school?
- How have the views of service users been used to inform the multi-agency provision available within the school?
- What does the school do to ensure there is good evidence for demonstrating the impact of multi-agency working on pupils' outcomes?
- How have multi-agency practitioners/professionals been involved in monitoring and evaluating the impact of their work within the school?
- What has the school leadership team done to raise awareness about the impact and work of multi-agency practitioners on-site?
- Is there any further support, advice, guidance or service provision the school wishes to commission from the LA or the Children's Trust?

It is useful for school and children's centre leaders and multi-agency service managers to look back at the seven questions at the end of the Introduction to this book. The multi-agency self-evaluation process will have provided good-quality evidence in response to each question.

Appendix

An introduction to the multi-agency self-evaluation process in Leafy Lane School

What does the multi-agency self-evaluation process comprise of?

There are nine aspects of multi-agency working which require evidence to be collected. These nine aspects are:

1. Policy, procedures and legal requirements
2. The workng environment
3. Leadership and management
4. Communication and information sharing
5. Inter-professional responsibilites and roles
6. Team working
7. Resources
8. Working with service users/clients
9. Professional learning

Benefits of engaging with the multi-agency self-evaluation process.

- Strengthens and improves collaborative multi-agency working
- Meets the Children's Workforce core standards
- Provides robust evidence for the SEF and OFSTED inspection
- Promotes the dissemination of good practice in multi-agency working
- Engages a range of stakeholders in the self-evaluation process
- Offers the potential to gain a national award in recognition of their good practice in multi-agency working.

What is involved in the multi-agency self-evaluation/award process?

- Purchase the handbook and download the resources
- Register with Every Child Matters (ECM) Solutions for the award
- Select a package of support and consultancy to suit the setting
- Make a payment for half the cost of the full award
- Deliver a presentation to key stakeholders on the process/award
- Undertake the audit of multi-agency working
- Produce an action plan
- Form a multi-agency working party/task group of nine members to gather evidence and review progress for their multi-agency aspect
- Nominate a lead senior member of staff for overseeing the process
- Build a multi-agency portfolio of evidence for each of the nine aspects

Time and cost implications of engaging
with the multi-agency self-evaluation process

- It can take a setting between 12 and 18 months to achieve the award
- Time needs to be allocated to the SLT member leading the process for monitoring and evaluating the overall process
- Time needs to be allocated to the nine people responsible for gathering evidence for each of the nine aspects of multi-agency working
- The cost of the award is at the lower end of national award pricing, which does not compromise the quality of the process
- Education settings can purchase additional support and consultancy
- Half the cost of the total award is paid on signing the agreement
- The final cost for the total award is paid on achieving the award
- The two stage payment spreads costs over two school financial year budgets

What type of evidence should be included
in the multi-agency portfolio of evidence

- **Documentary evidence**, e.g. minutes of meetings; reports; policies; evaluations from surveys; newsletters, media reports; data; information in leaflets
- **CD/DVD evidence**
- **School website extracts** relevant to multi-agency working
- **Photographs**
- **Audio recordings** and/or transcripts
- **Video Diary Room recordings** of stakehlders views
- **Extracts from cameos or case studies** relating to multi-agency working
- **OFSTED inspection report evidence**

What does a half-day assessment programme entail?

8.30	Arrival of the external assessor
8.30–9.20	Meeting with the head, Chair of Governors and SLT lead
9.30–10.00	Observation of multi-agency practice in action
10.00–10.30	Meeting with multi-agency practitioners observed
10.30–11.00	Meetings with a sample of multi-agency service users
11.00–11.30	Meeting with members of the multi-agency task group
11.30–12.00	Meeting with the Bursar, Administrative assistant, site manager
12.00–12.50	Lunch with children and snapshots of any multi-agency lunchtime activities
13.00–13.30	Feedback to the head and SLT lead for multi-agency working from morning's findings/observations

What a setting obtains on achieving the award

- A national award that is valid for three years
- A glass plaque
- A framed certificate
- A digital logo to use on education setting's stationery
- Inclusion on the Every Child Matters (ECM) Solutions website
- Opportunities to network and share best practice with other settings via the Every Child Matters (ECM) Solutions website
- An opportunity to apply for reassessment after three years to extend the award for another three years

Model school multi-agency partnership agreement

Statement of purpose

All the multi-agency professionals from Education, Health and Social Services, working directly with pupils, in partnership with the school, agree to provide accessible, good-quality, effective coordinated services, which help to remove barriers to learning and contribute to improving pupils' ECM outcomes.

The school welcomes and acknowledges the valuable contributions that multi-agency professionals make in helping to improve pupils' well-being. This partnership agreement clarifies the school and the services roles, responsibilities and expectations, in relation to the delivery of universal, targeted and specialist services to meet the needs of pupils and their parents or carers.

Each multi-agency professional working with pupils in the school agrees to complete and sign the attached partnership agreement. They also agree to comply with the school's Health and Safety, Safeguarding, Child Protection, Equal Opportunities, Confidentiality/Information Sharing, Whistle Blowing, Complaints and ECM policies and procedures.

The school is responsible for and will:

- Provide an appropriate accessible room(s) and a safe and healthy working environment.
- Provide access to administrative support.
- Promote the services to pupils, parents/carers and the community.
- Facilitate two-way communication between school staff and service professionals in order to share information.
- Listen to and act upon any multi-agency professionals' concerns or issues relating to service delivery within the school.
- Provide access to all relevant school policies and procedures.
- Offer opportunities to participate and contribute to inter-professional learning and development activities.
- Seek feedback from multi-agency professionals each year on how the school can further support or improve their work and service delivery.

- Report to the governing body on the effectiveness and impact of multi-agency service provision within the school.

The multi-agency service providers are responsible for and will:

- Deliver good-quality, effective services that meet the needs of service users.
- Inform the designated member of staff in school responsible for Child Protection if they have any concerns about the safety or well-being of a pupil they work with.
- Provide evidence of Criminal Records Bureau (CRB) checks (enhanced disclosure) and emergency contact information.
- Contribute qualitative and quantitative evidence to the school's SEF on the effectiveness and impact of their services and on pupil outcomes.
- Meet with relevant members of staff in school at least once per term or half term in order to review and assess service provision and pupil progress.
- Follow the relevant policies and procedures which relate to their work with pupils within the school.
- Undertake appropriate risk assessments where appropriate.
- Maintain relevant records to be made available to the school, which include a register of attendance, a record of provision/ services delivered, assessment and referral details.
- Ensure pupils are supervised and never left unattended during service sessions.
- Provide any specialist resources and equipment necessary for delivering their service.
- Ensure that any damage to school resources and facilities within the working area are reported and replaced or repaired, and that the working area is left in good condition after use.
- Inform the school in advance if they are likely to be absent or unable to provide their service on a particular day.
- Inform the Head of Partnerships for the school if there are any changes or disruption to service delivery.
- Complete an annual survey on the operation and management of multi-agency services within the school.

Please complete and sign the attached partnership agreement form

SCHOOL AND MULTI-AGENCY PARTNERSHIP AGREEMENT

School name: _____

This partnership agreement clarifies the roles, responsibilities and expectations of the School and Multi-Agency Provider in delivering services on the school site.

In accordance with the partnership agreement, _____
_____ (service provider), will deliver the following services:

Job title: _____ **Name:** _____
Nature of service(s) provided: _____
_____
_____
_____
_____

Date commenced: _____ **to** (end date) _____
Target group(s)/individual pupil(s): _____
_____
_____

School _____	Multi-agency provider _____
Name: _____	Name: _____
Position: _____	Position: _____
Signature: _____	Signature: _____
Email:_____	Email: _____
Phone: _____	Phone: _____
Date: _____	Date: _____

TO BE COMPLETED BY ALL MULTI-AGENCY PARTNERS WORKING IN SCHOOL

Please place a tick in the relevant boxes to indicate that you meet the following requirements. You will be requested to show evidence of how you meet the six requirements to the Head of Partnerships in school.

Name:_____ Agency/service: _____

Undergo regular health and safety checks ☐
Meet supervision arrangements for on-site activities ☐
Familiar with fire and emergency evacuation procedures ☐
Meet supervision arrangements for off-site activities ☐
Have a CRB Enhanced Disclosure Certificate ☐
Possess the relevant qualifications to undertake the role ☐

Glossary

Accountability refers to being answerable and responsible to someone for what is provided.

Additional needs describes children and young people whose well-being is at risk and who require extra support and provision from children's services.

Agency refers to any statutory or voluntary organisation.

Audit refers to a systematic and objective review that compares actual policy and practice against recommended criteria for established best practice.

Children's Trust is a local partnership which brings together organisations responsible for services for children, young people and families with schools in order to deliver better services to improve children's lives.

Collaboration refers to working jointly with others in order to achieve common goals.

Commissioning refers to securing and allocating resources to meet identified needs, and monitoring and evaluating the impact and outcomes of provision.

Common assessment framework (CAF) refers to the holistic multi-professional assessment process to assess the additional needs of children and young people who are achieving poor ECM well-being outcomes.

ContactPoint is an electronic information-sharing tool which enables multi-agency practitioners to find out who else is working with a particular child or young person, in order to prevent duplication or overlap in additional provision.

Continuing professional development refers to any training or activity which helps to improve the knowledge, understanding, skills and professional practice of those working with children and young people.

Disabled refers to any individual who has a physical or mental impairment which has a substantial, long-term adverse effect on their ability to carry out normal daily activities.

Early Years Quality Improvement Support Programme, introduced in September 2008, it helps LAs and leaders of early-years settings to improve the quality of their provision and services for children in order to align them with the principles of the Early Years Foundation Stage (EYFS).

Evaluation is concerned with gauging effectiveness, strength and weakness, and interpreting how well things are going.

Every Child Matters is a ten-year government initiative designed to improve children's and young people's life chances and well-being in five aspects: be healthy; stay safe; enjoy and achieve; make a positive contribution; and achieve economic well-being.

Extended services refers to the core offer of universal services provided by a school or children's centre from 8am to 6pm in order to meet the needs of children, young people, families and the wider community.

Information sharing refers to the process of passing on relevant information to other agencies, organisations and individuals that require it in order to deliver better services to meet the needs of children and young people.

Inter-professional working is when more than one agency or organisation works together in a planned and formal way.

Lead professional refers to any practitioner, usually from health, education or social services, who coordinates, monitors and oversees the multi-agency provision for children with additional needs. They also oversee the CAF process and act as a gatekeeper for information sharing.

Monitoring refers to checking progress against agreed targets, identifying any trends in performance or outcomes and ensuring that any national initiatives have been implemented.

Multi-agency working is when practitioners from more than one service or organisation work together, sharing aims, information, tasks and responsibilities.

National Service Framework offers a set of 11 quality standards for health, social care and some education services, which aim to reduce inequalities in service provision for children and young people.

Networking is the process where practitioners/professionals meet together periodically, for the purpose of sharing and exchanging ideas, best-practice, expertise and resources.

Outcomes refers to the identifiable (positive or negative) impact of interventions, programmes, initiatives on children and young people. It also refers to the five ECM well-being outcomes.

Practitioner refers to anyone working directly with children and young people and their families, who uses particular professional skills, knowledge and expertise in order to promote and improve their well-being.

Quality assurance refers to the systematic examination of the quality and the effectiveness of any service to ensure that provision is of good quality and meets the needs of service users.

Safeguarding refers to identifying children and young people who have suffered, or who are likely to suffer, significant harm and then taking appropriate action to keep them safe.

School Improvement Partner provides professional support and challenges to leaders of schools and PRUs, focusing on the quality and effectiveness of the school's improvement planning and self-evaluation processes.

Self-evaluation refers to the ongoing rigorous systematic information-gathering process, embedded in the daily work of the education setting, which gives a true and realistic assessment of its strengths and weaknesses.

Self-evaluation form gives a summary record of evidence, which assists Ofsted inspectors during the inspection of an education setting, helping to form a hypothesis about the quality and effectiveness of the provision available.

Stakeholder refers to any individual, group, organisation or institution that has an interest in a specific activity, project or programme.

Team around the Child refers to an individualised, personalised and evolving team of a few practitioners/professionals from different services who work and meet together in order to provide practical, targeted support to help an individual child or young person.

Transition refers to situations faced by children and young people which pose a challenge or change to their lives, e.g. a family bereavement, illness, divorce or break-up, moving on to the next stage in education.

Welfare refers to any child-safety or child-protection issues.

Well-being refers to having the basic things needed to live, be healthy, safe and happy. It also refers to the five ECM outcomes.

Whistle blowing refers to an individual who raises concerns and reports failures in duty of any practitioners working with children and young people.

Useful websites

www.cwdcouncil.org.uk

www.dcsf.gov.uk

www.ecm-solutions.org.uk – this website gives further information about the Multi-agency award, and the ECM standards award.

www.dcsf.gov.uk/everychildmatters – this government website is dedicated to ECM information.

http://lmscontent.ncsl.org.uk/ECM/flash.cfm – ECM Leadership Direct online resource. Click on 'Leading extended provision' then click to enter 'Multi-agency and partnership working'.

www.ofsted.gov.uk

www.standards.dcsf.gov.uk/nationalstrategies

www.surestart.gov.uk

www.tda.gov.uk

www.teachernet.gov.uk

www.teachers.tv/video/22456 – *School Matters: Every Child Matters & Multi-Agency Working*

www.teachers.tv/video/3407 – *Secondary Support Staff: Multi-Agency Working*

References and further reading

Barker, R. (2008) *Making Sense of Every Child Matters: Multi-Professional Practice*. Bristol: The Policy Press.

Cheminais, R. (2007) *Extended Schools and Children's Centres: A Practical Guide*. Abingdon: Routledge.

Cheminais, R. (2008) *How to Achieve the Every Child Matters Standards: A Practical Guide*. London: SAGE Publications.

Cheminais, R. (2009) 'Getting together' *Special*, January 2009 (15–17).

Cheminais, R. (2009) *Effective Multi-agency Partnerships: Putting Every Child Matters into Practice*. London: SAGE Publications.

Coleman, A. (2006) *Collaborative Leadership in Extended Schools. Leading in a Multi-Agency Environment*. Nottingham: National College for School Leadership.

Craig, J., Huber, J. and Lownsbrough, H. (2004) *Schools Out: Can Teachers, Social Workers and Health Staff Learn to Live Together?* London: DEMOS/Hay Group Education.

CWDC (2006) *Your Induction to Work in Children's Social Care: A Workbook for those Working with Children, Young People and Families*. Leeds: Children's Workforce Development Council.

CWDC (2009) *The One Children's Workforce Framework*. Leeds: Children's Workforce Development Council.

DCSF (2008) *What is a Children's Trust?* Norwich: Department for Children, Schools and Families.

DCSF/NCSL (2008) *The National Standards for School Leadership*. Consultation Paper. Nottingham: Department for Children, Schools and Families, and National College for School Leadership.

DfES (2007) *National Standards for Leaders of Sure Start Children's Centres*. Nottingham: Department for Education and Skills.

DfES/DH (2004) *National Service Framework for Children, Young People and Maternity Services*. London: Department for Education and Skills/Department of Health.

GTC (2007) *Inter-professional Values Underpinning Work with Children and Young People*. Joint Statement. London: General Teaching Council for England.

Her Majesty's Government (2005) *Common Core of Skills and Knowledge for the Children's Workforce*. Nottingham: Department for Education and Skills/Department of Health.

NCSL (2008) *Every Child Matters (ECM): The best of ECM Leadership Direct*. Nottingham: National College for School Leadership.

NCSL (2008) *ECM Premium Project: School Leadership, Every Child Matters and School Standards. Levers for Leaders and Learning, a Toolkit for Leadership Development in Extended Schools*. Nottingham: National College for School Leadership.

Ofsted (2008) *Inspecting Extended Schools and Children's Centres: Guidance*. London: Office for Standards in Education, Children's Services and Skills.

Siraj-Blatchford, I., Clarke, K. and Neeham, M. (2008) *Team Around the Child: Multi-agency Working in the Early Years*. Stoke on Trent: Trentham Books.

TDA (2007) *National Occupational Standards for Supporting Teaching and Learning in Schools*. London: Training and Development Agency for Schools.

TDA (2007) *Professional Standards for Teachers: Qualified Teacher Status*. London: Training and Development Agency for Schools.

TDA (2007) *Extended Services. Toolkit for Governors*. London: Training and Development Agency for Schools.

TDA (2008) *School Improvement Planning Framework*. London: Training and Development Agency for Schools.

Index